Holocene Pointbreaks

Previous collections by Jake Goetz

meditations with passing water (Rabbit, 2018)

Unplanned Encounters: Poems 2015–2020 (Apothecary Archive, 2023)

Holocene Pointbreaks

Three Drifts: March 2020—March 2021

Jake Goetz

PUNCHER & WATTMANN

First published in 2024
Published by Puncher and Wattmann
PO Box 279
Waratah NSW 2298

https://www.puncherandwattmann.com
web@puncherandwattmann.com

ISBN   9781923099142

Cover design by David Musgrave
Typesetting by Morgan Arnett
Printed by Lightning Source International

A catalogue record for this work is available from the National Library of Australia

Australian Government

Creative Australia

This project has been assisted by the Australian Government through Creative Australia, its principal arts investment and advisory body.

Acknowledgements

I'd first like to acknowledge the traditional owners of the lands on which I live and write, the Gadigal people of the Eora Nation. I pay my respect to their elders past, present, and emerging.

Excerpts from this work first appeared, sometimes in a much different form, in *Plumwood Mountain*, *Cordite*, *Rabbit*, and *Overland*. A shortened version of 'A tracing' (from the first section, 'By a drowned valley estuary') was shortlisted for the University of Sydney's David Harold Tribe Poetry Prize (2023), and the suite, 'Coastal heath compost' (from the second section, 'Whaletalk'), was shortlisted for *Overland*'s Judith Wright Poetry Prize (2022).

This book was completed for a Doctor of Creative Arts degree at The Writing and Society Research Centre, Western Sydney University. It was supported by an Australian Postgraduate Research Training Program scholarship. I give thanks to my supervisors, Kate Fagan, Ivor Indyk, and Helen Koukoutsis for their invaluable feedback during the writing process.

Lastly, I would like to thank David at *Puncher & Wattmann* for seeing this book to print, and also Eva for her feedback.

Contents

By a drowned valley estuary

... the ['Cooks'] river lacks a definite beginning as well as end. It is deprived of narrative continuity, and hence a clear identity. An unbroken human connection is lost. Even today, the extension of bike paths along the river has only partly overcome this truncated state ... On these, one has to leave the riverbank and later re-join it, travelling the last section – mostly away from water – towards the river mouth past Barton Park and Muddy Creek, part of it in an area where the river never flowed until the 1950s.

—Ian Tyrrell, *River Dreams* (2018)

1   A layering

     urging the tide
   toward Strathfield

  a pale moon
pinned to a sheet

of blue   lapping
  water against

  a sandstone
     arrangement

          *

    gently rising
  southward the land
   an abstraction
     red tiles and bricks
      windows and cables
      dissected by fences
       weathered by years
      of occupation

          *

upon a
cement patch

three pelicans
sculpted by
the weather

heads wind-
twisted   warm-
tucked beneath wings

*

where mangroves
are christmas trees
decorated in the tinsel
of blue green and pink
plastic bags

*

stretching out
its wings
one pelican waddles
into mud
opens its
mouth
as if to howl
at clouds

rearranging sky
        rippling through
water's black

        *

through wavelengths
of sun the eyes
confine to blue

so the things one
thinks and sees
are not always

to be believed
but a layering
of windows

augmented
if not cracked
by culture

in time

2   A body

tracing river's curve
backyard fences col-
lapse with the in-
different gesture
of topography

*

at the water's
serrated steel
edge   a mother
and three kids

point at mullet
flexing vertebrae
to leap   catch sun
glisten like sheets

of aluminium

*

grazing like cattle
ibis press their feet
into a cricket oval

in a window
a man stands
like a stockman

of the inner-city
sipping coffee

*

an old bloke
rides a bike
pulled by a pony
leashed to his handlebars

from the speaker
in his basket   Bob Marley
competes with a ride-on mower
a whipper-snipper

mudlarks and cockatoos
the engines stopping
fuck bro i dunno
there's alodda whippin to do

splashing back down
as leaping
mullet home in more
than an idea

*

in a weeping bottlebrush
    a fallen red gum
  rests at an angle

  new growth shoots
from its exposed roots
    and here i am

    a body
through which
  the world lives

  or the world lives
and for which there is
    this body

3   A tracing

in a clouded
oaken wash

morning cool
and olive

a coffee
makes an atlas

of the body
warming stomach

with the tierra
sol y rios

de Colombia

*WARNING
DO NOT EXCAVATE
SHELL – S.M.P.
HIGH PRESSURE
OIL PIPELINES*

pumping petrol
between Clyde and Gore Cove
the airport and Kurnell
Newcastle and Yenangyaung

where the resource
naturally rises to earth's surface
and for which the British
invaded Myanmar in 1885
taking control of their
oil industry and establishing
the petrol empire
Burmah-Shell

*

a pebble path
lined with sheoaks
leads to *Burial Vaults*

an empty mausoleum
cut from a rock shelf
for Sydney business tycoon

and one time politician
Thomas Holt   a man who built
a Gothic mansion

on the hill above in 1857
on *one of the most beautiful sites
in the district*   12 acres stocked

with rabbits   alpacas
and other exotics

but upon Holt's death

the land subdivided
and the building bought
by a French order

of Carmelite nuns
eventually evicted
for outstanding debts

at which point
the land transformed
into a WWI artillery range

and after the war
the mansion torn down
to build houses

for returning soldiers
one of which my opa would rent
in the early 60s

a fitter and turner
a child once programmed
by the fascist jingles

of the Hitlerjugend
13 at war's end and just 22
when he boarded a ship

in Bremerhaven
and spent a year working
the steelworks at Port Kembla

then came the move
to Newtown where he met
an Irish Catholic

recently arrived from Belfast
via London

*

a group of kids
push out
in a makeshift raft

and in a pram
on the shore
i think

to my father
beside the nawi
carved from

sandstone
in an ode
to the Gadigal

and Wangal
to the failure
of erasure

in the colony's
tanneries abattoirs
and wool washers

Bulanaming
this place
a kangaroo

hunting ground
stretching north
to the Harbour

*

by a bridge
that was once a dam
built to provide
fresh water
for Canterbury's
Sugar Works (est. 1841)

made of local ironbark
and sandstone   the factory
processed raw sugar
from the Philippines

transported here
by horse and cart
from the CBD

but in 1854
the factory doors closed
due to a labour shortage
triggered by the Gold Rush
and around that time
the water so polluted
some people who went in
for a swim died of typhoid

*

a flock of little black cormorants
sit on a rectangle of land that juts
into an artificial harbour

a pelican glides   throws out
its legs   wings extended   rocking
its body left to right

on the winds of association
a paratrooper bracing to land
in the DMZ

the way culture shapes
our speak   places Martin Sheen
in a kayak with an AK47

de-stabilises one's senses
from the immediacy of the thing
the pelican crashing down

startling the cormorants
that launch into the water
creating wakes for mud crabs

to assess   everything
endless in discussion
as downriver

almost hidden amongst sheoaks

this is Cadigal Wangal Country
baram, guwagu, barrabugu
yesterday, today, tomorrow

4   A date

tinged strawberry
Starburst pink
morning sun swims
through puddles
that return
the soccer field
to a wetland
ibis rippling
eucalypt reflections

*

by 'Cup and Saucer Creek'
potassium cyanide memories

December 1973   12,000 gallons
pouring out Sunbeam's plating plant

in the following days
15 tons of dead fish collected

in the following weeks
thousands of dead birds

the cost to Sunbeam
$3000

*

somewhere around
Croydon Park
the tide peters out
between cement slants
as water turns east
in search of sea

a route which
during the last ice age
was twice its length
and flowed across the land
that covered Kamay (Botany Bay)
where it met the Tucoerah (Georges)
and Deeban (Hacking) rivers
before emptying out
several kilometres east
of today's coastline

*

standing beneath
a pre-colonial ironbark
working with the wind
to rain cotton-candy pink
onto the path

across from

an industrial estate
the stream draped
in fluorescent green algae

*

freshly cut pine
packed in cubes
mirrors a row
of brick houses

a wetland nearby
recently re-built
to filter out
'storm water'

ibis walking
among regenerated
flax lily and
common rush

*

as the ABC relates
today 250 years since
two Gweagal (Dharawal) men
yelled 'warra warra wai'
at the Endeavour floating
toward the shore

warra warra wai

(you're all dead)

'when the two men
opposed the landing
   they'were protecting
the country in a spiritual way
  from ghosts'
     —Ray Ingrey, Dharawal elder

a Gweagal shield
  with a bullet hole
now sitting in the British Museum
  in London

The British Museum states
it is 'suggested and not confirmed'
  that the shield belonged
to the [Dharawal] warrior Cooman
  when he was shot at
  by Cook's landing party.

'We are still waiting
to get that shield back'
 —Theresa Alder, Gweagal
  and Yuin woman, believed to be
  the descendent of Cooman

*

seeping through
Strathfield Golf Course

at the end of the green
from behind a fence

i watch the water
disappear

onto the railyards
of Chullora

5   A refraction

wind blurs green
to glass and metal
a Campbelltown train

rattling yellow
through mud
and mangroves

i pedal across
the Princes Highway bridge
(where the river's

first dam was built
to provide drinking water
for a population of
approx. 30,000 people

completed in 1842
by a chain-gang of 500 convicts
as well as unemployed men
paid in rations of meat and sugar

but the dam demolished
between 1896 and 1899
due to an increase
in pollution and flooding)

from Gameygal
to Bediagal Country

*

TINIES VERSION
scrawled along a rail bridge

two pelicans
huddled on an island

where hundreds of Catholics
in religious celebration

once made a tradition
of ferrying the Portuguese

pilgrim statue
Our Lady of Fatima

an island created
by the footstep

of the Goolay'yari
(Pelican) Dreaming

(remember riding
the Illawarra line as a kid

the banner that read
      SAVE FATIMA ISLAND)

      another dreaming
  from the Dharawal

          describing the river
              as the landing place

          of the Guwarra
          (Humpback Whale)

          *

      By Tranquil Waters

      or the Concordia
      German club

      a golden light
      through trees

      a group of
      white boys

      bathing naked
      and 'free'

Sydney Long's
symbolist vision

of beauty
wrestling with

a post-storm
average of 13.8

million micro-
plastic particles

   *

beeped off
   the path

a council worker in a ute

   sprays pesticides
into oaken feet

   *

sun carves
a glinting river into
   the Alexandra Canal

named for a Welsh princess
in the dream of Sydney
as a Birmingham

of the south
the *aim* to connect the river
north to the Harbour

and south via Muddy Creek
to Kogarah's market gardens
in 1896 the skeletal remains

of a 6000 year old dugong
unearthed here alongside
stone tool fragments

and in 1885 alone
362 tons of 'night soil' was dumped
on a weekly basis

by rogue carters from
Surry Hills and Redfern
Waterloo and Alexandria

*

in the dream of Sydney
as a Los Angeles
del sur a pyramid of earth

sits by the road

a billion dollar
network of tunnels
built to cut just minutes
off people's commutes

*

beneath the M5
like a geyser in Yellowstone

a rectangular pool
foams sulphuric yellow

*

between long rows of

bokchoy

an old woman squats

stands

adjusts her conical hat

*

three black cockatoos
ride the westerly
following a section
of river altered
for Sydney Airport

between 1947 and 1955
the river's lower reaches
were diverted 1.6 km west

of their natural outlet
allowing for the reclamation
of mangroves mudflats
and saltmarsh

this area had been relatively
isolated from development
and was a distinct ecological zone
home to the Cooks River Prawn
and migrating waders who flew there
from their far northern breeding grounds

*

from the seven gaping mouths

of a bridge   the river meets

a clean stretch of cool sand

at Kyeemagh   small clear waves

refract sunlight as water fades

to a light grey blue darkening

as it edges to bay's heavy tones

*

standing on the break wall
a fisherman reels nothing in

behind him at La Perouse
a network of steel breaks apart the sky

another man sitting on a rock
sips a VB in the sun

in the early days of the pandemic
no planes landing   a southerly

brushing sand along the beach
near the spot Cook purported he *found*

a very fine stream of fresh Water in 1770
a place *where the Ship might lay almost*

land-locked and wood for fuel may be got
everywhere   a place where in 1788

Watkin Tench noted a village
which contains more than a dozen houses

and perhaps five times that number of people
their raison d'etre more clearly evoked

by W. Clements   a First Fleet officer
as we advanced up the river numbers of natives

seemed fishing in their canoes
while others were dressing fish on the banks

they ran away on our peoples' approach
howling and making a strange noise

they were observed for the first time to have dogs
they are of the wolf kind with long shaggy hair

when they found our people did not molest them
they ventured to come near in their canoes

and when the boats were returning down river
they ran after them upon the beach

and sometimes stopped abreast of the boats
calling out   as usual   Warraw!   Warraw!

the country was here observed to be very low
and marshy   but very fit for growing rice

Whaletalk

*That great America on the other side of the sphere, Australia, was given to
the enlightened world by the whaleman ... The whale ship is the true mother
of that now mighty colony. Moreover, in the infancy of the first Australian
settlement, the emigrants were several times saved from starvation by the
benevolent biscuit of the whale ship dropping at anchor in their waters.*

—Herman Melville, *Moby Dick* (1851)

*Underwater, sounds can take half an hour to bend around the horizon. Or
they can fade in a matter of seconds. Sounds constantly arrive from different
spaces and times. And somehow whales decipher an acoustic world where the
past and present arrive all at once.*

—Ellen Garland, *Fathom* (2021)

1   Windlogue

like an intangible
flock of albatross
morning wind slams
against the Carbon-
iferous windshield
of the range

offering a way
to trace the coast
down past
Yuin rivers
that pour
into beaches
flanked by
Holocene
pointbreaks

as if the ocean
were a mouth
the seabed lungs
and cars hauling up
the Princes
a bassline of drums
beating to the migration
of the Pacific Humpback

or recall that flag
once flown above
Sydney's observatory
which read 'JB'
to inform the city
the southerly had reached
Dharawal Country
(Jervis Bay)

the same observatory
in which colonial astronomer
William Dawes
sought to understand
the Gadigal language
speaking with Patyegarang
and speaking out when
Gov. Phillip ordered
First Nations deaths
after Pemulwuy speared
Phillip's game keeper
down by Kamay

where morning
watches the tide
ease from the mouth
of a drowned valley

at Kyeemagh beach
where wind weaves
a quilt from sand
carrying the poem
off into canyons
of glass and cement
to break branches
from figs and eucalypts
or imagine itself an ibis
lifting rubbish from
over-flowing bins
if not water whipping
into a Manly Ferry
lashing commuter legs
all the way to Awabakal

2   Coastal heath compost (1)

feet track cool morning sand
as waves break through open air
and bees heave pollen between
bright orange banksias   small pools
of green algal forests   yellow robins
darting across a ti tree atmosphere
that sweet honey scent roots walk back
to the absolute centre of the sudden
to a patch of white sandstone
pushed up through earth's skin
like exposed bone   if not the Permo-
Triassic kneecap of a diprotodon
christened with the blow of a Corona bottle
a raven's caw caught in the engine
of a *SINGAPORE AIRLINES* 747
sky's steel baleen sustained
by the nutrients of a krill-like capital
the coastal heath tremoring body up
through Salvos second-hand boots
their memory a Vietnamese bull
bled out in a factory on Saigon's outskirts
where to walk upon some sense
in the constant sensation of movement
in the commercial nature of each continuous moment
in which lies the point of some kind of poetry
or a point   at least   from which it extends

3   Whaletalk

iron-oxides river
reds and creams
between ridge-
lines of grey rock
shaped by wind
and salt   a kid
at the cliff's edge
pointing out

as a black curve
emerges like a hill
only to dissolve
back into
the sedimentary layers
of an oceanic geology

but bursts
and sudden   and crack open
body airborne   to fall   the ocean
in its tonnage   stomach   like concrete
twists a white sun   throwing white
debris to seagulls
that fall to
the breach

to people
that cheer
not unlike the
centre of a universe
contemplating itself
throwing arms to sky
or holding screens

to catch to catalogue
a spray of sea mist
splashing like
the atmospheric feet
of a lifeguard
fat with summer krill
migrating to bask
and give birth
in the warm waters
near the equator

or near to extinction
their bodies once used
for oil and baleen

i.e. to illuminate
lamps that lined
Parisian streets

British candles
that flickered ruby
through sherry glasses
in London drawing rooms

Russian soaps
and perfumes
washed into
the Volga

whips cracked
across a history
of slavery
in Louisiania

pesticides sprayed
into Japanese
rice paddies

or a corset pressed
against a woman's chest
as she walks past whalers
on the piss in the Rocks
and notes the stench
of the fishery
at the site of today's
Opera House
wafting across the quay
into *The Fortune of War*

4   Coastal heath compost (2)

through fire's gnarled submission
to Sculpture by the Sea   banksias burnt back
stretch west to the Caltex oil refinery
white tree-trunk tanks filled with the sap
of a Saudi desert   a memory of union picnics
beneath Norfolk Pines at Gunnamatta
or a family huddled around a mid-winter heater
watching Channel 10 to spot their father
a fitter and turner   walking the Bridge chanting
workers united will never be defeated
or those defeated evenings having worked
around-the-clock during a shutdown
how he'd fall onto the couch covered head-to-toe
in deep time   open a Toohey's Old like T.S. Eliot
measuring life out in warm spoons of petroleum
a family fed by fossils turned to fuel   to money   to war
to a brick house on the corner of two tar roads
down the street from Miranda Fair
where arborists routinely cut figs and eucalypts
shaping them around power lines
that routinely electrocuted fruit bats
a rusted pipeline crawls beneath a barbed wire fence
as two sulphur-crested cockatoos soar
UNDER 24 HOUR SURVEILLENCE

5   The meeting place

drawn into a gully
of red gums   moth larvae
competes with *PLJ*
GORAN <3 SAW
TY DARREN

a *Dharawal (Cabbage Palm)*
the tree's bud cooked and eaten
the leaves used to weave bags
baskets fishing lines and nets
the straight trunks once
hollowed out and used
as troughs and drain pipes
in the early days of the colony

at *THE MEETING PLACE*
a sandstone obelisk
erected by Thomas Holt
a man who once secured
a lease over an area
of Dharawal Country
which stretched from
Sutherland to Cronulla
and which he named Miranda
after a character from
Shakespeare's *The Tempest*

clear turquoise water
lapping against
the first oyster-clad rocks
the British stepped upon

in the distance
a FedEx plane taxis
across the tarmac
while a freighter docks
at the wharf

a metal sign relays
the natives resolutely disputed
the landing   although they were
but two   and we thirty
or forty at least

we parleyed with these two
for a quarter of an hour
but they remained resolute
so a musket was fired over them
the effect of which was that
the youngest dropped a bundle
of lances on the rock   however
he snatched them up and both
renewed their threats and opposition

a musket leaded with small shot
was now fired at the eldest
who was about 40 yards from
the boat   it struck him on the legs
but he minded it very little
so another was immediately fired
and on this he ran to the house
about 100 yards distant
and soon returned with a shield

in the meantime
we had landed
on the rock

across the road
among shopfronts
a family sit outside
Captain Cook's Take Away
eating fish 'n' chips in the sun

6 Coastal heath compost (3)

by water's edge on Gweagal land
a memorial stone for *FORBY SUTHERLAND*
the Endeavour's poulterer *THE FIRST
BRITISH SUBJECT TO DIE IN AUSTRALIA*
at 'Kurnell' and so wrote Kendall
*'Tis Holy Ground! / That soul, / the first for whom
the Christian tear / Was shed on Austral soil,
hath heritage / Most ample!* as time drives out
past remnant sand dunes mined to oblivion
freckled kids sliding boogie boards into a future
of vaseline fucks in the backs of station wagons
at 'Green Hills' now a suburb of white cubes
a homogenous ode to capital's ubiquity
yet contradictorily more reminiscent
of that social housing project passed on a bus
in Northern Argentina each mudbrick chimney
printed with the head of Guido Fawkes
or Che Guevara another week another bus
stopped at dawn somewhere near Bolivia
burning oil drums a banner held up
*COMUNIDAD INDIGINA DE VARAS
TENEMOS DERECHO A UNA EDUCACION DIGNA
SALUD SEGURIDAD CAMINOS Y EDIFICIOS*

7 Whaletalk (2): a Yuin Country coda

La Niña makes
a construction site
of morning   hammering
watery nails into palms
spread like a tarpaulin
between red gums
still black and bare
from summer's fires

later   at Eden Harbour
we watch a crane
drive pylons into water
rippling clouds that rub
the body from a distant
mountain   leaving
just a tip   a pyramid
pinned to atmosphere

in a Norfolk Pine
we hang an umbrella
and boil water
on a Kmart cooker
by a *HERITAGE SITE*

whaling by Europeans
commenced in Twofold Bay
in 1791   with the first
shore-based whaling station
est. by Capt. Thomas Raine
here at Snug Cove in 1828

the industry then led
by the Imlay family
and later the Davidsons
who using rowboats
worked with orcas
on their baleen hunts

the orcas paid
for their work
with the delicacy
of lip and tongue
leaving the carcass
for the whalers
which included
local Yuin people
who weren't paid
in currency but with
tobacco and provisions

their reward
for the long-standing
tradition they shared
with the orcas
as Oswald Brierly noted
during his time managing
Ben Boyd's pastoral
and whaling operations

The natives of Two-
fold Bay regard the killers
as incarnate spirits
of their departed ancestors
and in this belief they go
so far as to particularise
and identify certain
individual killers

a practice once
appropriated for
'Old Tom' *a highly*
extroverted orca
that would swim up
to the Davidson's station
and lash the water
with his tail to notify
the crew his pod had
cornered some baleens

but only 20 years later
Tom's pod began to disappear
wiped out due to industrial
whaling or because around
the same time the local Koori
were taken off their land
and sent to missions

the whale carcass
even once believed
a cure for rheumatism
in 1892 the *Pambula Voice*
reporting   *male patients were put*
in the whale in a nude condition
while females were covered in a gown
they then remained in the whale
for about an hour and a half
the temperature of the carcase
being 105 °F (40.5 celsius)

the most remarkable cure
effected by the treatment
was the case of a man from Bega
when he first arrived in Eden
he was obliged to walk with sticks
but after one trial of the treatment
he was so much benefiter
he was able to walk back to Bega

Dr Eddie of Bombala
was very favourable impressed
with the results of this method
which he compared to a huge poultice
opening the pores of the skin ...

that afternoon
at Bittangabee Bay
in a national park
named after Ben Boyd
a Scotsman who once
kidnapped 192 people
from Tanna and Lifu islands
and forced them to work
his pastoral operations

in the north   clear water
rivers turquoise through
bright purples and reds
piled at the headland
by an ancient volcano

while in the east
sunlight pales
as the campfire
peels the skin
from logs
year by year
turning to ash

to sky   to somewhere
in time immemorial
or is it better to say
outside *time*
inside First Nations
Dreaming   that whales
were first woven into
poetry   or better to say
outside *poetry*   inside
Djeeban's sandstone headland

that Guwarra
i first saw as a kid
photographed in its body
Billabong boardies
and a Mambo t
sunscreen blotched
on freckled cheeks

The coal coast

Our kind is suffering, in this world and the next. If we ever get to heaven, they'll make us work the thunder.

—Georg Büchner, *Woyzeck* (1837)

Our age builds enormous reservoirs of power, formless
as the tensing stress it extracts from everything.
It doesn't know temples anymore.

—Rainer Maria Rilke, 'The Seventh Elegy' (1923)

1 'Welcome to the Black Diamond District'

at Sandon Point
grey rain blurs ocean
to dense cumulus

as a surfer traces
the slow undulations
of swell

cuts back to the memory
of a 200 metre jetty
that once stretched out

to the horizon
where red coal ships now sit
and can be squeezed

between fingers
like toys the US Army
once dropped into villages

during the Vietnam War
for the festival of *Tết Trung Thu*
into communities they bombed

only shortly before
the Range stretching north
in sporadic sun bursts

a glistening wet blanket
heaped at the continent's edge
by the restless sleep

of tectonics   if not a wave
waiting to break
on houses of weatherboard

and brick   front lawns
that gently slope to tar rivers
that feed the highways

*

down on the beach
a lifeguard moves flags
out with the tide

a woman prods seaweed
with a stick and i think
to D.H. Lawrence

jotting down in his notebook
men women and children pick
sea-smooth pebbles of coal

in one place where the beach
is a black slope   or maybe standing
on this headland when he wrote

as a rule the jetty on its poles
straddling a little way into the sea
was as deserted as if it were

some relic left by an old invader
but then it had spurts of activity
when steamer after steamer

came blorting and hanging
miserably round   *like cows to the cowshed*
on a winter afternoon

built by the Bulli Coal Co.
in 1863   the jetty also once used
            to transport 'blacklegs'

between the Bulli pit
            and the ships that conveyed
        them from Sydney

        the company having refused
to negotiate with the union
        over piece-rate hours

        and wages which fluctuated
with the uncertainty
        of the market

                              *

on January 17 1887
upon word that 40 blacklegs
were to arrive at Bulli jetty

a general roll-up began
and by 6 o'clock the muster was on
a good war footing

the group numbering some 400
or 500 persons
(including about 150 women)

the excitement rose to fever height
as the steamer came close
and several heads

which were supposed to have
black-legs under them
could be seen on board

these invaders were then piled
into a locomotive
but upon the train

reaching the town
collective Bulli was found
in 'solid square'

on the tramway
and as the locomotive whistled
and screeched

the square only became
more solid and impregnable
while one woman

with Joan of Arc-like gesture
stood upon the railway gate
and defiantly waved a red flag

screaming 'DANGER!'
and yet nearer and nearer came
the iron-horse

but closer and closer
stood the stone-wallers
volleying forth broadsides

of verbal jeers
theatre and pleadings
while the local engineer

having run the engine up
to the crowd hesitated to knock
persons down with it

and so an engineer from Sydney
 took charge   but he too dared not
 run it into the crowd

 or over the front rank of women
some of whom placed their feet
 before the engine wheels

 to defy Captain Pollock
of the iron-horse   they being on
 the Queen's highway

and fighting for their husbands' rights
 but then after about
 half-an-hour of squabbling

 36 of the enemy jumped out
of the waggons and surrendered
 to the Bulli army   the engine taking

 the other 4 back to the jetty
and some months later
 the strike 'settled'

the less radical miners signing rules
 stipulating reduced piece rates
 as well as the rigid management

of employees e.g.
Rule 6—Interference by employees—
any employee interfering

in any way with the orders
issued by the colliery manager
or his overman

for regulating the work of the mine
shall be liable
to dismissal without notice

and later that month
at 2:30pm   on March 23 1887
the Bulli pit exploded

killing 81   the only survivor
17-year-old Herbert Cope
who at the time

was walking out from the mine
considered lucky
to have only been flung

against a pit prop
and knocked unconscious
the source of the explosion

*was in the headings known
as 'Hill End' which were known
to be gassy and subject*

*to gas 'blowers' and although
safety lamps were in use
apparently it was common*

*to remove the safety gauze
from around the flame
to permit more light*

*to emit from one's lamp
as this was the miners'
only light source*

*

Excerpt of *The Bulli Colliery Accident Royal Commission*
Minutes of Evidence, 13 May 1887
John Barnes Nicholson, Bulli Miner, sworn and examined

      3634. From what you know
of the mine since the strike,
    have you heard anyone remark

    that there was a large
accumulation of gas there?
       I heard several men mention it;

one in particular. It was Jerry Westwood.
    3635. Where did he work?
    In No. 2 heading.

    3636. What did he say?
He told me that night, at Bulli
    I think it was the Friday night week

    before the explosion—
that they had struck a heavy blower
      that day in the heading,

which was giving off gas all day.
    3637. What did he say?
    He remarked it was a very heavy blower,

and said they could hear it whistling
100 yards away. 3638. Did you make
any remark? *I asked him if there were*

any men working round about him
with naked lights and he said there were.
I said, 'God help you;

one of these days you will get it.'
3639. Were you secretary
of the Union at that time? *I was.*

3640. Having heard
of that enormous escape of gas
did you take any action? *I did not.*

3641. Did you not bring it
under the notice of the Association?
I did not. 3642. Did you consider it

your duty to do so? *I did not.*
3643. Why? *I believe the management*
were thoroughly aware of it at the time.

3644. Did you believe
what Westwood told you?
Was he a truthful man—

I had no reason to doubt his word.
3645. A blower giving out such
      an enormous quantity of gas

would be a very dangerous element,
      would it not? *Yes,*
   undoubtedly it would be if there

     was not a sufficient quantity
of ventilation to carry it away.
   3646. Did you know

that the men were working
in its vicinity with naked lights?
     I was told that that was the case.

3647. That would be another
     element of danger, would it not?
  Yes; particularly for those

   on the return side.
3648. And it was imperilling lives
  of all working there?

  It would depend on the quantity
of gas coming off. 3649. A blower that
     could be heard 100 yards away

must have given off
        a considerable quantity of gas,
      was that not in itself a danger?

      It might be dangerous to the parties
working there, but I do not believe
     it would be to the other portions

     of the pit. 3650. Holding
the responsible position you do,
      and being the leader of others,

did you not think it was your duty
      to take steps to avert
    such an evil as that?

     l did not think I had any right whatever.
3651. Not from a motive of humanity?
     It was purely a matter of business.

     3652. I am asking you to take it
from a human point of view.
      You knew that numbers

of lives were being held as by a thread,
      did you not think it your duty,
    as a responsible officer,

to bring that state of things
under the attention of the management or Union?
With regard to our own Union,

I believe that every man in the Union knew it.
I also knew that the manager knew it,
and if I thought that any communication

from me would have altered it,
I should have been very glad
to have made it, I can assure you;

but l had every reason to believe
that every man in the pit knew of it,
for it was a matter

of common conversation.
3653. But no steps were taken
to avert it?

Every man was afraid to do anything,
for fear of losing his work. 3654. Why?
Because of the rules that were signed

after the strike.

2   Coal frags (1)

at the site
of Xiahe house
in China's Shaanxi
Province   coal fire
remnants dated
3490 BC

in the Awabakal's
stringy bark canoes
small fires kept burn-
ing with the coal
they call nikkin

3 to 4000 years ago
burned in funeral
pyres across the
damp green fields
of Wales

a passion too for the Romans
who exploited as much of Britain's coal
as possible   but when their Empire fell
the fuel remained buried   almost forgotten
until the Medieval period   and even then
King Edward I   for his hatred of the sub-
stance   saw it banned in his kingdom in 1306
torturing hanging and decapitating those who
broke the law   but a growing England needed fire
and her forests were becoming exhausted   and so
the English became the first nation to burn coal
on a large scale   leading John Evelyn to note
in 1661 that coal-fired London resembled
'the suburbs of Hell'

3 Stumbling upon Geera

what can a butter
of sunlight smeared on a leaf
tell us about morality

or family? that the underside
is a night one can't differentiate
from morning?

or if i filled a bag
with pebbles
from the Yangtze

and told you to take them
to the end of the sky
would you find walking

bottomless? or collapse
from exhaustion?
could you watch

the way words float
through years
only to get stuck somewhere

on an escarpment
in a mess of lantana and flax
drawing meaning out

from the senses
that are already meaning
in their essence

to try locate the self
in some planetary
syntax of symbols

in search one might say
to let letters loose of logic
or to a logic let loose

of letters   opting instead
for simple transfers
tensing muscles in blood

like ferns in soil
to strain legs
ground a branch

stumble upon
a giant grey ironbark
rooted beside

a brick chimney shaft
which channelled air down
to the Kemira Colliery

where coal was cut
     from Mt. Kiera
    loaded onto wagons

    and driven
to Wollongong port
   along this track

   i now walk
tracing a coal path
     through Country

*

in 1982   hundreds
of workers faced
the sack at Kemira

and so 31 miners spent
16 days underground
while mass demonstrations

filled Wollongong's streets
and trains took thousands
of workers to Canberra

where they protested
the apathy of the Fraser government
broke past barricades

stormed Parliament's steps
and kicked through the doors
chanting 'we want jobs'

as one miner relayed
I was stuck in the middle
and I was trying to get out

and I couldn't
I was just going in
everyone was just going in

it was like water down the sink
I even heard coppers saying
'stick it into 'em'

coppers!

*

Kemira Colliery Coal Works Fatalities

1871: John Cole
(fall of roof stone)
1871: John Coombes (Cole?)

(fall of roof stone)
1879 May 14th: Joseph Seal
(roof fall)

1880 Sep 24th: Thomas Allum
(run over by wagon)
1884 Sep 6th: Andrew Bell

(fall of coal)
1885 Nov 14th: Thomas
Dumphy (fall of coal)

1887 Jan 30th: Thomas
Danby (fall of coal)
1888 Oct 4th:

Robert Kenning (run over by set)
1896 Aug 28th: James
Goldrick (wagon on incline)

1897 Sep 13th: Charles
Benjamin Drew (crushed
between wagon buffers)

1900 Oct 15th: Patrick Hayes
(natural causes) 1906 Jul 10th:
John Dobing (runaway skip)

1906 Sep 20th: John Dumphy
(roof fall) 1908 Aug 31st:
William McDonald (trip and fall)

1910 Mar 4th: Thomas
Francis O'Brien (heart failure)
1910 Mar 17th: Frederick

Peterson (roof fall)
1912 Jan 19th: John Charles
Wilson (fall of roof stone)

1915 Jun 17th: Joseph Hay
(roof fall) 1930 Apr 15th:
Frederick Walker

(fall of roof stone)
1939 Sep 18th: Antonio Carollo
(died from injuries)

1948 Nov 8th: Harold
Whitehead (electrocution)
1949 May 25th:

Keith Arnett (crushed between loco
and tipping ramp)
1950 Mar 28th: Eric James

(crushed upon slipping
under the coal cutter)
1951 Nov 15th: Walter

Hurt (collided with
a derailed mine car)

*

through a break
in trees   the Gong fog-
faded green

kilometres squared
by houses and industry
the Pacific's blue hands

massaging the beach
like toes on the feet
of some anthropo-

centric hill   but still
what it is to marvel
at a view   to unravel

a stone block
cracked and cast out
from the escarpment

to unanchor ideas
in a waving
or rolling as rising

or recalling
everything balanced
by water   land a leaf

eaten away
by the oceanic mouth
of a caterpillar

as rain falls like fingers
onto keys of leaves
and a cicada rings out

through the humidity
a South Coast nocturne
welcoming La Niña

back to this coast
a flash   red and green
shifts   takes form

protracts wings and
descends over trees
stuck to the hills

like old cereal to a bowl
a female lyrebird
running to a sign

The Illawara Escarpment
was called Merrigong in the early days
of white settlement

a place where *The west wind*
        Oolaboolawoo lived
    with his six daughters

       Geera

             Clematis

                    Wattle

                        Lilli Pilli

                            Wilga

                                Mimosa

    a place the sign says
may have been a place of massacre
   with no further details

   no Royal Commission
'a massacre' near a carpark
    where four people

eat chips with dip
      their bodies hunched
   over screens

   'a massacre'
and then the disemcoalment
   of Geera   her stomach-

energy loaded onto ships
and for 135 years they dug
and across Merrigong still dig

4   Coal frags (2)

in the 18th century England's love of coal
became threatened by the depth of their mines
which routinely flooded   and so in 1710   an iron-monger
Thomas Newcomen   invented a device that burned coal
to produce steam which powered pumps that extracted
the water   decades later   James Watt would improve
Newcomen's design with Matthew Boulton
(who   when once asked by King George III
how he made his living   replied 'I am engaged,
your Majesty, in the production of a commodity
which is the desire of kings'   to which the King asked
'just what do you mean?'   and Boulton replied 'Power,
your Majesty')   later still   Watt would create the first
mobile steam engine with William Murdoch   transforming coal
into a transport fuel and the West into an Industrial Revolution
a time in which 5/6 of earth's coal was mined in Britain and which
in 2000   atmospheric chemist Paul Crutzen would seek to label
the advent of the 'Anthropocene'

not long after Watt's creation   in 1796   in the shipyards
of Calcutta   the Bengali built boat *Begum Shaw* was renamed
Sydney Cove and stocked with 31,500 litres of alcohol (mostly rum)
sacks of rice   sugar   tea   tobacco   salted meats   Chinese ceramics
barrels of tar   casks of vinegar   footwear   soaps   candles   textiles
a musical organ   a horse-drawn buggy   cattle   horses and chickens
manned by a crew of 44 Bengali sailors and 5 Englishmen
they set out on their southern journey only to be met by heavy seas
off New Holland's west coast   springing a leak that required the ship's
pumps to be used continuously   then near Van Diemen's Land
on the verge of sinking   they beached on Preservation Island
and built a shelter from the ship's timbers   next   13 Bengalis   Clarke
Thompson and Bennet set off in a longboat across the Bass Strait
in search of Port Jackson only to be wrecked 4 days later on Kurnai land
thereafter forced to continue by foot through Bidwell Yuin and Dharawal
Countries   aided by some Indigenous   confronted by others   1 Bengali
killed during a conflict   another 11   as well as Thompson and Bennet
dying on the northward journey   it not being until 6 months after
leaving Calcutta   having walked 600km over 77 days   that just 1
Bengali and Clarke were spotted by a ship at Wattamolla south
of Sydney   and upon their arrival in the colony   Clarke recounted
his journey to Governor Hunter   noting he saw
a significant amount of coal in the cliffs just south of
the settlement   and in July that same year   George Bass
while surveying the coal deposits   came upon the skeletal
remains of Thompson and Bennet and went on
to name the area   Coalcliff

5   This way 2 death →

        winding through rows
of sun warmed weather-
     board worker's cottages

     i come upon a bowlo
with solar panels   *BAR*
        BISTRO FOX KENO

on a wooden veranda
      a couple drink tea
    watching their child play

     in a European garden
next door   a former miner's
    clubhouse   old brick

    cottage crumbles
its roof rusting a deep
      iron red

then up the road
     at Windy Gully
   yellow flowers grow out

    from graves
feeding off the bodies
    of men and children

harpooned like whales
for energy

*

on July 31 1902
261 men and boys
were mining coal

in the Kembla Colliery
including 15-year-old clipper
Alexander Morrison

who was moving skips
along the tunnels
when the roof in the 35 acre goaf

near the 4th right fell
liberating flammable gas
into a rush of air

that blew through the tunnels
to mix with coal dust
and the naked light

of 17-year-old Henry Morrison's
head lamp   igniting
an explosion that tossed skips

and blew straight out
the entrance   flinging wood rock and metal
into the workers outside

meanwhile   in nearby Kembla Heights
the miners' families felt
        the earth move

saw sky turn black
        watched birds flee
    across the mountains

        while underground
some miners didn't hear a thing
    and continued working

    as carbon monoxide filled
the tunnels   killing more
            than the initial explosion

eventually   70 men appeared
            from the Manager's adit
    as the tunnel entrance

        had collapsed
another 84 found
    their own way out

    and another 96 were killed
with more to die later
        from the effects

taking the toll over 100
        the 19-year-old wheeler
    Michael Brennan

    who had started
at the mine just 4 days earlier
    the only body never recovered

    from Australia's worst
industrial 'accident'
        and just 8 weeks later

on September 24th 1902
    work at the mine
    recommenced

*

walking between
moss-washed rocks
and fern-thick slopes

giant figs and cedars
are but small remnants
of rainforest

along a fire trail
i follow traces of coal
to a watering hole

covered in green algae
a place ponies drank
before being whipped

behind wagons
a sun-flash of iron
collapsed red bricks

by a road
a guard rail painted
this way 2 death →

climb a fence
rusted green iron sheds
long brick buildings

lantana growing
through smashed windows
into a kitchen

cabinet doors ripped
from hinges
a blue bong painted

on a wall
a sink on the floor
the material legacy of

*

after the explosion
the *Sydney Morning Herald* reported
the colliery *was one of the best*

ventilated mines in the State
the *Illawarra Mercury* also stating
gas had never been known

to exist in the mine before
the site's manager
William Rogers convinced

the mine was absolutely
without danger from gases
a Royal Commission concluding

gas and coaldust
were responsible
for the explosion

6   Coal frags (3)

in New York   1856
Eunice Foote   an American
scientist (and the 8th signatory
to the Declaration of Sentiments)
became curious about whether
certain gases might affect
the composition of our atmosphere
and so conducted an experiment
placing thermometers in two glass cylinders
she then extracted the air from one while filling
the other with different gases   from this she discovered
the one with CO_2 trapped the most heat   concluding
that an 'atmosphere of that gas would give to earth
a high temperature' but her discovery (which she was
unable to present at the 1856 American Association for
the Advancement of Science's 8th annual meeting
due to her gender) was largely written out of history
when Irish physicist   John Tyndall   just 3 years later
conducted a similar experiment   a man today
considered the father of climate science

today it's estimated
that between 1751 and 2019 coal-related CO_2
emissions rose from 9,350,000 to 14,360,000,000 tonnes
an increase noted to have contributed to earth's average temp-
erature rising 1.0 degree over that same period   which in turn
has increased extreme weather events   i.e. cyclones droughts floods
intensified La Niñas prolonged El Niños fires that burn through
places that have never burnt before   e.g. in the Amazon   which in
2019 lost 906,000 ha   while in June that same year fires scorched
24 million ha in Australia over 11 months   until May 2020
when California went aflame and lost 1.8 million ha
while Siberia at the same time lost 26 million   and in 2011
Australia became the first nation to put a price on carbon
an attempt   however inadequate   to urge fossil fuel industries
to lower their emissions   but two years later it also became
the first to can it   and then came a decade of Liberal governance
a political party whose attitude to coal is perhaps best summarised
by a moment in 2017   when Scott Morrison   who would go on
to become Australia's PM   took a piece of coal into parliament
proclaiming   *this is coal   don't be afraid   don't be scared   it won't hurt you*
it won't hurt you   it's coal   it was dug up by men and women who work
and live in the electorates of those who sit opposite … it's coal that has ensured
for over 100 years Australia has enjoyed an energy competitive advantage that
has delivered prosperity to Australian businesses and has ensured that Aus-
tralian industry has been able to remain competitive under a global market
MR SPEAKER   those opposite have an ideological   pathological
fear of coal

7   At Mt Kembla Lookout

above the coastline
the steelworks stands
like an industrial Amazonas

transpiring coal
into dense grey clouds
that sail in

from the Pacific
as i sail out with a rip
to the East Australian Current

winding its way south
and east to Aotearoa
before linking with

the South Pacific Gyre
and flowing on to Chile
where it traces up

the Peruvian coast
only to loop back
to the Reef

upwell off ancient
submarine volcanos
transfer nutrients

from the depths
to water's surface
where phytoplankton

photosynthesise   sequester
carbon   provide half
of earth's oxygen

and create the gas
that helps create clouds
and the rain

which falling now
drags land's nutrients back
into its embrace

a self-feeding system
punctured by
the steady hum

of the highway below
our very own
deep time song

echoing through
suburban streets
    to fill a stadium

of atmosphere

Vergangenheitsbewältigung: a note on writing the text

I first began this book in March 2020, at the crossroads of two vastly
different socio-ecological crises, the Black Summer bushfires and the
COVID-19 pandemic. Though these two events are not *overt* subjects of
the three 'drifts' gathered here[1], they played an indelible part in shaping
the composition and thematic preoccupations of the work. Indeed, they
should be credited for prompting me to undertake a more localised rumi-
nation (restricted as I was by lockdowns) on the global environmental crisis,
pushing my thinking beyond sweeping planetary gestures of 'oneness' and
into a more nuanced, historical critique of the ongoing ecocidal narrative
that continues to play out on First Nations lands in Australia.

Fusing a longform ecopoetic practice with the psychogeographic tech-
niques of *dérive* and *détournement*—first coined by twentieth-century
French Marxist theorist, Guy Debord—this book continued my interest in
reworking Debord's playful modes of Marxist inquiry into a type of ecopo-
etic methodology.[2] A poetic practice that is not only interested in excising
the residue of 'capitalism and bureaucracy' by reimagining spaces beyond
the 'metro, boulot, metro, dodo' of everyday life, but in interrogating the
anthropocentric mentality which arguably stands as capital's guiding force.[3]

Despite this self-proclaimed drifting approach, one which had 'no preset
route or duration' and which was 'driven by intuition rather than calcu-

---

1   A suite of poems in response to the Black Summer bushfires were, however,
published in my second book, *Unplanned Encounters: Poems 2015–2020* (Apothecary
Archive, 2023).

2   My first book, *meditations with passing water* (Rabbit, 2018), a work which
traced the socio-ecological history of the Maiwar (Brisbane River), implemented a
similar psychogeographic approach.

3   Debord, Guy. "Theory of the Derive." *Internationale Situationniste #2*, 1958.

lation',[4] during the process of composition, these drifts found themselves drawn deeper and deeper into the histories of three resources key to the colonial project in Australia—water, whales and coal. Once I'd completed the project, I was quite surprised to see the way in which, when read as a whole, the book doubles as a fragmented (and oft sequential) history of the early years of settlement, starting with Cook's encounter with a river in 1770, the establishment of the whaling industry in the early 19th century, and the advent of coal mining in the mid-late 19th century (and its continuation into the 20th century and the present day). This focalisation on resource extraction has since led me to think of the work as somewhat synonymous with Elena Gomez's idea of a 'Marxist Ecopoetics': the creation of 'a site at which the relations between capitalism, labour and ecology can be comprehended in a specific and expansive way'.[5]

Another central writer and thinker driving my historically focused Eco-Marxist experiment in poetic composition, or poetic *composting*, was Waanyi author, Alexis Wright, who in her essay, 'Politics of Writing', reflects

> Writing is about crawling down the hole to see what we have all inherited. It is about dragging our memories, realities and losses back up to the surface and letting the whole world see them in the full, glaring light of day. This is what Günter Grass also said is the reason for writers such as himself who grew out of Nazi Germany. He said, our work will become memory, preventing the past from coming to an end. For only then can the wound be kept open and the much desired and prescribed forgetting be reversed ... (18-19)[6]

---

4   Ibid.

5   Gomez, Elena. "Coal Flower Aesthetics." *Overland*, iss. 246, 2022, online.

6   Wright, Alexis. "Politics of Writing." *Southerly*, vol. 62, iss. 2, 2002, pp. 10-20.

Perhaps it was not only as an Australian but a German (by descent) that I was drawn to the way Wright references Grass (a former Waffen-SS soldier of all things) when identifying the need for writers not to allow history to become eaten up and obfuscated by the present. This provocation no doubt played a significant role in shaping this work, making me question how I, in my own creative practice, might be able to ensure the present and future remain not only in conversation with the past, but enmeshed in its continual unfolding. To turn to Grass himself, perhaps I wanted this book to be an example of his *Vergangenheitsbewältigung*—a 'coming to terms with the past'. Yet, as a *settler* in the context of an *unceded* Australia, another question undoubtedly arose: how could I 'crawl down the hole and see what we have all inherited' without misrepresenting First Nations People or misappropriating their language, history, culture, and knowledge?

For me, this wasn't something I could simply set out to 'do' and 'achieve' on my own, especially in the context of COVID-19, and so I chose to focus on us(urp)ing specifically *colonial* texts and events in this text. During the writing process, however, I did frequently come upon information (through both research and public signage) which spoke directly to First Nations continuing connections to Country. Having encountered this material, I decided it would be tantamount to a colonial erasure to allow information already in the public domain to remain buried beneath my own ecologically-focused interrogation of colonisation, especially given the digressive, out-in-the-world nature of my writing-as-recycling practice. For these reasons, I chose to include certain materials that I felt allowed my own attempts at conjuring a more demythologised history of Australia's socio-ecological relations to be further *decolonised* by the work of First Nations People who have worked tirelessly to have their voices heard, and who have been kind enough to share their cultural knowledge and history with non-Indigenous Australians.

Below is a detailed list of First Nations terms and materials included in the book. A second list for non-Indigenous references follows.

p. 10: 'nawi' is a Gadigal word for canoe. The nawi the poem directly talks to is a sandstone sculpture created by Murrawarri artist, Joe Hurst. It is by the river's edge close to the Illawarra Road bridge in Marrickville. The Gadigal term that follows, 'Bulanaming', was drawn from Ian Tyrrell's *River Dreams* (2018, New South Publishing). Meaning 'Kangaroo hunting ground', the word was used to describe the Country that stretches from the 'Cooks River' north to the Parramatta River.

p. 13: The metal plaque that reads *this is Cadigal Wangal Country / baram, guwagu, barrabugu / yesterday, today, tomorrow* lies near the nawi mentioned above. It was placed there as a joint project between the Marrickville Aboriginal Consultative Committee and Marrickville Council.

p. 16-7: On this particular morning I came upon an article on ABC News that alerted me to the fact it was the 250th anniversary (28th April 2020) of Cook's landing at Kamay. Being at the 'Cook's River', and being the first time I'd actually read an Indigenous account of that 'first contact', I felt it paramount to include a paraphrased version of this article in the poem. This was less to do with 'writing' an Indigenous perspective and more to do with creating space within my work to allow the Indigenous perspective to speak for itself. The article was written by the ABC's Indigenous affairs correspondents, Isabella Higgins and Sarah Collard, and can be found here: https://www.abc.net.au/news/2020-04-29/captain-cook-landing-indigenous-people-first-words-contested/12195148. More recently, on 23 April 2024, Trinity College and the Museum of Archaeology and

Anthropology (MAA) finally agreed to repatriate the Gweagal spears to the La Perouse Aboriginal Community. They will be displayed at a new visitor's centre at Kamay, Kurnell.

p. 20-1: The reference to the 'Guwarra and Goolay'yari' D'harawal Dreaming was drawn from the following website, https://dharawalstories.com/, created by D'harawal knowledge holders, Frances Bodkin and Gawaian Bodkin-Andrews. I have not recounted these Dreaming stories here as they are not mine to tell. They can, however, be read and reflected upon on the website.

p. 35: I was first alerted to the story of Patyegarang and her encounter with William Dawes by William Davies' *26 views of a Starburst World* (UWAP 2012). I learned of Bidjigal warrior Pemulwuy's spearing of Phillip's game keeper, John McIntyre, from the SBS documentary, *First Australians* (2008), written and directed by Arrernte and Kalkadoon film maker, Rachel Perkins.

p. 42: The information detailing the colonial use of the 'Cabbage Palm' was drawn from a sign on the Banks-Solander Track in Kamay National Park. It was placed there by the NSW National Parks and Wildlife Service.

p. 43-4: This story of 'first contact' is presented on a sign by the obelisk which commemorates Cook's landing. It reproduces an extract of Sir Joseph Banks' journal detailing the events of April 28th 1770. I have made some stylistic edits here and there. The main reason for its inclusion was to contrast it to the ABC article paraphrased on p. 18, thereby exposing just how little the colonisers understood of the Gweagal people they were attacking. Banks's reference to a 'house' further unsettles the idea of *Terra Nullius*.

p. 69: The Awabakal term for coal, 'nikkin', and information pertaining to its use, were drawn from the University of Newcastle's 'Hunter Living Histories' project: https://hunterlivinghistories.com/dreaming/.

p. 81: This text was drawn from a sign atop Geera/Djeera (Mt. Kiera) which was written to accompany a sculpture titled, 'The Six Daughters of the West Wind' (2007), created by Alison Page, a First Nations artist from La Perouse, and a non-Indigenous artist from Melbourne, Tina Lee. These two artists collaborated with other local Aboriginal artists, including Lorraine Brown, Narelle Thomas, Jodie Stewart, Val Law, Alison Day, Phyllis Stewart, Bonny Foley-Brennan, Lila Lawrence, and Debbie Hamstead-Callaghan. The artwork is comprised of 'six differing sized bronze structures or "Gunyas" and cast from twigs collected on the site. The structures identify each of the six daughters of the west wind.' An excerpt of the sign has been reproduced in the poem with the permission of the artists. In December 2023, Wollongong City Council announced their support for Djeera and the Five Islands to receive Aboriginal Place recognition by Heritage NSW.

References

By a drowned valley estuary

Ian Tyrrell's *River Dreams* (2018, NewSouth Publishing) was an indispensable resource in the writing of this poem. Much historical information was drawn from his work (see pages 16, 17, 22-23, and 25), though no direct quotes were used. Additional historical information was drawn from the sources listed below (and are most often highlighted by *italics*). I also note that in some cases I have edited these excerpts so as to better ingrain them within the poem.

p. 8: Ghosh, Amitav. "History." *The Great Derangement.*
The University of Chicago Press, 2016, pp. 100-4.

p. 8-9: "History Lost: The Warren." *Marrickville Heritage Society*,
31 Aug. 2014, https://marrickvilleheritage.org.au/2014/08/31/
history-lost-the-warren/.

p. 11-12, 19: Witton, Vanessa. "Damming the Cooks River."
The Dictionary of Sydney, State Library of New South Wales, 2013,
https://dictionaryofsydney.org/entry/damming_the_cooks_river#
ref-uuid=0fd492d4-2db7-a0b0-539f-c682a563d3fe.

p. 22: Long, Sydney. *By tranquil waters*. 1894. Oil on canvas on
hardboard. Art Gallery of NSW, Australia.

p. 22: Hitchcock, James. "After a storm, microplastics in Sydney's
Cooks River increased 40 fold." *The Conversation*, 29 May 2020,
https://theconversation.com/after-a-storm-microplastics-in-sydneys-
cooks-river-increased-40-fold-139043.

p. 25: "SYDNEY AIRPORT 1947 – 1975.", *Adastra Aerial Surveys*, 12 Oct. 2011, https://www.adastra.adastron.com/projects/sydney-airport-1947-1975.htm.

p. 27: Cook, James. "Cook's Journal (May 1770)." *National Museum of Australia*, https://www.nma.gov.au/exhibitions/endeavour-voyage/cooks-journal/may-1770.

pp. 27-8: Muir, Lesley. "Aboriginal people of the Cooks River valley." *The Dictionary of Sydney*, State Library of New South Wales, 2013, https://dictionaryofsydney.org/entry/aboriginal_people_of_the_cooks_river_valley.

Whaletalk

The italicised texts in this section were drawn from signage encountered during the writing process. The last poem, 'Whaletalk (2): a Yuin Country coda', draws extensively from information gathered at the Eden Killer Whale Museum (Eden, NSW), as well as a snippet from the following newspaper article on 'Old Tom':

pp. 48-9: Foden, Blake. "Old Tom: Anniversary of the death of a legend." *Eden Magnet*, 17 Sep. 2014, https://www.edenmagnet.com.au/story/2563131/old-tom-anniversary-of-the-death-of-a-legend/.

The poem 'coastal heath compost (3)' uses lines from Henry Kendall's sonnet, 'Sutherland's Grave' (1869). The English translation of the last 3 lines of this poem roughly read as follows: 'THE INDIGENOUS COMMUNITY OF VARAS: WE HAVE THE RIGHT TO A DIGNIFIED EDUCATION, HEALTH, SECURITY, ROADS, AND BUILDINGS'.

The coal coast

Italicised texts in this section were drawn from the following sources, as well as from signage I came across while writing. As per the first section, some of these excerpts underwent editing but I have chosen to retain italics to emphasise the collaborative nature of the piece.

pp. 57-8: Lawrence, D.H. *Kangaroo*. Martin Secker, 1923.

pp. 59-61: "A Bulli Bannockburn (*Illawarra Mercury*, 18 Jan. 1887)", in Organ, Michael, "The Battle of Bulli: Women, Children & Striking Coalminers repel Blacklegs, Police & a Steam Locomotive at Bulli, New South Wales, Australia." *Illawarra Unity*, vol. 2, iss. 4, 1999, https://ro.uow.edu.au/unity/vol2/iss4/4/.

pp. 61-3: Dingsdag, Don. *The Bulli Mining Disaster 1887*. St Louis Press, 1993, http://mineaccidents.com.au/uploads/bulli-explosion-1887.pdf.

pp. 64-8: "Bulli Colliery Accident, Report of Royal Commission: together with the minutes of evidence and appendices." *New South Wales Legislative Council*, 1887, https://www.resourcesandgeo science.nsw.gov.au/__data/assets/pdf_file/0013/1141042/Bulli-Colliery-Accident-Report-of-Royal-Commission.PDF.

p. 69: "Coal." *Geoscience Australia*, https://www.ga.gov.au/education/classroom-resources/minerals-energy/australian-energy-facts/coal.

p. 69: Venkat Ramani, Raja. "Coal Mining." *Britannica online*, 1998, https://www.britannica.com/technology/coal-mining.

p. 70, 83: Flannery, Tim. *The Weather Makers*, Text Publishing, 2005.

pp. 76-7: Southall, Nick. "The Wow factor: Wollongong's unemployed and the dispossession of class and history." *Illawarra Unity*, vol. 8, iss. 1, 2008, https://ro.uow.edu.au/unity/vol8/iss1/8/.

pp. 74-5: Zubrycki, Tom. *Diary of a Strike*, Kemira Productions, 1984. Documentary. https://vimeo.com/173879112.

pp. 76-8: "Kemira Colliery." *Illawarra Coal*, 2018, https://www.illawarracoal.com/minebase/minebase-d-1/300-kemira-colliery.html.

p. 84: "The Sydney Cove and her impact on early colonial exploration." *Naval Historical Society of Australia*, March 2018, https://navyhistory.org.au/the-sydney-cove-and-her-impact-on-early-colonial-exploration/.

p. 84: McKenna, Mark. "Sydney Cove shipwreck an epic tale of adventure and survival in 1797." *ABC RN*, 30 May 2017, https://www.abc.net.au/news/2017-05-30/survival-story-sydney-coves-shipwrecked-sailors/8536714.

pp. 87-9: Lee, Henry. "A Reflection on the Mt Kembla Disaster." *Illawarra Unity*, vol. 3, iss. 1, 2003, https://ro.uow.edu.au/unity/vol3/iss1/8/.

p. 87-9: "1902 Mount Kembla Coal Mine Explosion." *NSW Resources Regulator*, 2022, https://www.resourcesregulator.nsw.gov.au/safety-and-health/events/learning-from-disasters/learning-from-disasters-timeline/mount-kembla-1902.

p. 92: "Mt Kembla – Mine Accidents and Disasters." *Mining Accident Database*, 2022, http://www.mineaccidents.com.au/mine/90/mt-kembla.

p. 93: Shapiro, Maura. "Eunice Newtown Foote's nearly forgotten discovery." *Physics Today*, 23 Aug. 2021, https://physicstoday.scitation.org/do/10.1063/pt.6.4.20210823a/full/.

p. 94: Ritchie, Hannah, & Max Roser. "CO2 emissions by fuel type." *Our World in Data*, 2020, https://ourworldindata.org/emissions-by-fuel.

p. 94: Morrison, Scott. "Scott Morrison brings a chunk of coal into parliament." *The Guardian*, 9 Feb. 2017, https://www.theguardian.com/global/video/2017/feb/09/scott-morrison-brings-a-chunk-of-coal-into-parliament-video.